Elephants

by Grace Hansen

Abdo
ANIMAL FRIENDS
Kids

abdopublishing.com

Published by Abdo Kids, a division of ABDO, PO Box 398166, Minneapolis, Minnesota 55439.

Copyright © 2016 by Abdo Consulting Group, Inc. International copyrights reserved in all countries. No part of this book may be reproduced in any form without written permission from the publisher.

Printed in the United States of America, North Mankato, Minnesota.

052015

092015

 THIS BOOK CONTAINS RECYCLED MATERIALS

Photo Credits: iStock, Shutterstock

Production Contributors: Teddy Borth, Jennie Forsberg, Grace Hansen

Design Contributors: Laura Rask, Dorothy Toth

Library of Congress Control Number: 2014958397

Cataloging-in-Publication Data

Hansen, Grace.

 Elephants / Grace Hansen.

   p. cm. -- (Animal friends)

ISBN 978-1-62970-893-5

Includes index.

1. Elephants--Juvenile literature.   I. Title.

599.67--dc23

2014958397

Table of Contents

Elephants

Wild elephants live in Africa.

They also live in parts of Asia.

4

Elephants are very big. They can weigh up to 14,000 pounds!

Elephants have long noses called trunks. They also have big floppy ears.

Elephants love to eat grasses and fruits. They also eat **roots** and bark. They use their trunks to eat.

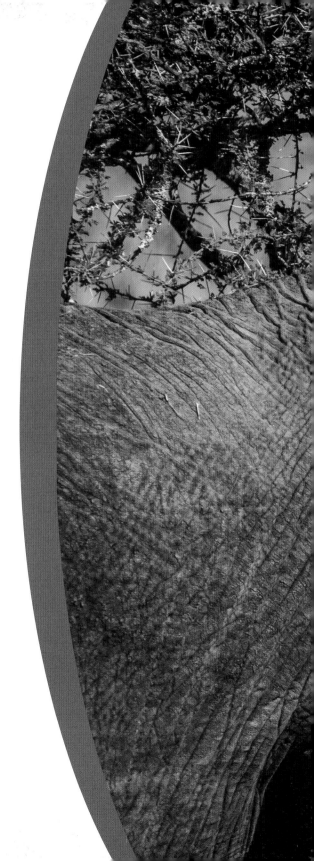

Leading Ladies

Elephants live in groups

called herds. The oldest

female leads each herd.

She is called the **matriarch**.

Herds count on **matriarchs**.

She knows the area the best.

She knows where to find

food and water.

Sometimes a herd feels **threatened**. In this case, the herd circles around the **matriarch**. They **protect** her from harm.

Kind & Caring

If one member is hurt, the others know. The herd will move slowly. This is so the hurt elephant can keep up.

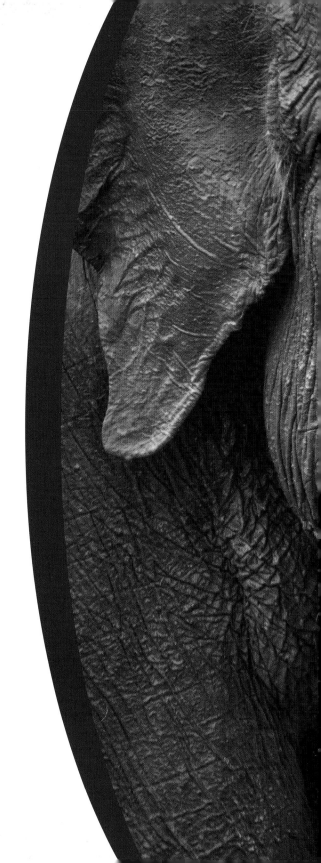

Elephants are kind and amazing animals. They care for one another.

20

More Facts

- African elephants have a great sense of smell. It is the best in the animal kingdom.

- Elephants are very **sensitive**. They feel loss. They mourn dead elephants.

- Elephants can recognize themselves in mirrors. Not many animals can do this.

Glossary

matriarch – a female, usually the oldest, who rules a group.

protect – to keep someone safe.

root – the part of a plant that grows underground.

sensitive – able to quickly and easily feel or notice.

threatened – to fear being harmed by something else.

23

Index

abdokids.com

Use this code to log on to abdokids.com and access crafts, games, videos, and more!

Abdo Kids Code:
AEK8935